# Instagr

# Beginners:

# Learn The Basics of Instagram, Get More Likes, Attract New Followers Guide

By

Joseph Joyner

# Table of Contents

Instagram For Beginners: Learn The Basics of
Instagram, Get More Likes, Attract New Followers
Guide

By Joseph Joyner

# Introduction

You might be wondering, what is the buzz with all the vintage looking photos in the internet. Why is everyone uploading gloomy selfies? If you haven't heard it yet, then let me introduce you to INSTAGRAM. It's a groundbreaking application and social networking site that changed how we view photographs. If you think a cup of coffee, your backyard or maybe your slippers is not a picture perfect then think twice because INSTAGRAM can help you transform usual photos worth sharing with the world. This book will be your vital guide to INSTAGRAM.

# Chapter 1. What Is Instagram?

INSTAGRAM is a popular social networking application that makes sharing your photos and videos from your smart phone easy and fun. With over 300 million monthly active users, INSTAGRAM has gained massive popularity and undoubtedly became one of the most loved social networking sites of our generation.

It paves way to mobile photography and gives us the notion that everything can be photographed. It is best known for its unique filters and easy to use editing tools that allow you to capture ordinary photos and make it look extraordinary.

# Chapter 2. Why Do People Love Instagram?

INSTAGRAM revolutionized photo blogging and it is by nature that people love and appreciate visuals. It may targets photographers and artists, but its appeal is general. And to ask why people love INSTAGRAM may also sound like "Why do people love pictures?"

## a. ONLINE PHOTO ALBUM

INSTAGRAM makes sharing your photos and videos to your family and friends for free, fast yet fun. You can use it as your online photo album with a creative twist. It allows us to capture our memories whether it's a cup of coffee in a rainy afternoon or your new shades for the summer; you can make it artistic with a little help of filters.

## b. PERSONAL BRANDING

Whether it is business or personal branding, INSTAGRAM can help you to make a look that matches your personality through focusing on visuals. It can be an online portfolio for artists, photo-blog for retail shops and more.

### c. SALES AND MARKETING

It is a good channel for businesses to promote their brands, increase sales leads and boost marketing. In a generation where everyone is online, it's not a question anymore why businesses and brands should also build a strong online presence. It enables businesses to showcase its creative side through photos and videos that celebrates their brand identity.

### d. ONLINE INFLUENCE

INSTAGRAM has over 300 million and counting users making it one of the best social networking sites to gain and influence people. You can build a network for your niche, reach a certain group of people and make a good advocacy here. Public figures use it to connect with their fans and even advertisers and PR agencies use it to launch new campaigns.

# Chapter 3. How To Use Instagram?

INSTAGRAM is free and simple. It is a chronological thread of photos that facilitates easy sharing, liking and commenting. To jump start, follow the instructions below.

## Step 1: Download It

To create an INSTAGRAM account you have to first download it to app store. Just type "INSTAGRAM" in the search bottom, select it, install and launch.

INSTAGRAM is free and accessible in IOS, Android and Windows devices. It is also accessible in the web but it doesn't permit you to upload photos and videos.

## Step 2: Register / Sign Up

After you launch INSTAGRAM you need to register to start using it.

Click the SIGN UP button.

You can manually enter your e-mail address or you can simply sign up by connecting to your other social networking account. Either ways is suggested; it is just up to you which you find more convenient.

INSTAGRAM will also ask you to fill the username and password.

**TIPS FOR USERNAME**

Your username plays a crucial role to your account to be easily discovered. Your followers will use this to mention you so try to make it memorable yet cool.

POINTS TO REMEMBER: Keep your password strong and avoid using your username as your password. If your INSTAGRAM is linked in your other accounts and your password is hacked, then this may result to online identity thief.

**PROFILE PHOTO AND BIO**

You can upload your photo and it will be cropped into a circle, so make sure your photo will still look good in circle. You can add a 150-word for your personal bio and indicate your website as well. To make a good first impression to your followers keep your bio straightforward, irreplaceable and cool. Avoid being too serious and stiff, remember that this is a social networking site not a curriculum vitae.

Here are some of samples to inspire you in writing a witty and memorable Instagram bio.

1. FOR PHOTOGRAPHERS:

"Photographs are my alphabet."

2. FOR SELFIE COMPILATION:

"A selfie tells a thousand of other selfies I deleted before I finally choose the best one."

3. FOR FOOD BLOGGERS:

"Imagine life without food. Now that is a form of suicide."

**FOLLOW YOUR FRIENDS**

To follow your friends, you can optionally import contacts from your contact list from your other social networking accounts. By following people, you can see their posts in your newsfeed and you can like and comment to it.

You can follow anyone in INSTAGRAM as long as their account is public. If they are in private mode, you can still click follow, but this is still subject for the approval of the user.

## Step 3: The Tabs

**How to start using INSTAGRAM?**

Good thing, INSTAGRAM is a very simple social networking site. You don't need to be intimidated and overwhelmed by it, just familiarize the following basic tabs for easy and convenient navigation.

**a. HOME AND NEWSFEED**

**(Home Icon)**

This is where you can see the photos and videos of the people you follow. You can scroll the posts, like it by clicking the heart sign or just simply double tap the photo and comment by clicking the speech bubble sign. The "3 vertical dots" in the right side under the photo gives you the option to report the photo if it's inappropriate.

To refresh or reload your Newsfeed you can simply scroll down from the top most of your feed. And to load more of the previous posts, just click the "plus sign" under the thread whenever you reach the bottom.

## b. SEARCH AND EXPLORE

## (Magnify Icon)

This allows you to browse photos and users base on the photos you like, users you follow and popular photos in your area.

You can use the SEARCH BAR above to look for specific users or hashtags. If you wish to follow a celebrity and there are lots of accounts in the results, follow the account with a VERIFIED SIGN. This sign is a "blue check" that you can see after the name of the user and it means that this is the legit account.

## c. TAKE A PHOTO/ VIDEO

## (Camera Icon)

So you are done building an impressive and catchy profile and you're now excited to post your first INSTAGRAM post.

Here is how to begin.

INSTAGRAM allows you to share a one photo at a time and one 15-seconder video by clicking the "camera icon". When you click it, you can either choose to upload from your gallery, or take a photo or video. The photos and videos you share are square, so choose a picture that compliments the square shape.

For videos, you can shot a video of a minimum 3 seconds and maximum of 15 seconds video. Just tap the "VIDEO" tab and start recording.

TIPS FOR YOUR FIRST POST:

Don't know what to post? Okay, first is to ask what your overall theme in your account is. Is it a personal account? a documentary of your life? Celebrity photos? flavors of ice creams? or your travel bucket lists?

Then from that you can get an inspiration for your first post.

Here are some specific suggestions you can try.
1. Take a selfie to introduce yourself and don't forget to add a cool caption.

2. Take a photo that represents your niche. Examples: (Coffee, pizza, paint brush, guitar, drums, books etc.)

After you choose your photo, you can now proceed to enhance it by applying a filter.

## What Are Filters?

Filters are what make INSTAGRAM a hit because it allows a variety of options in editing your photos. This allows you to enhance your photo and video so take your time to choose a good one.

## Filter

You can click MANAGE to arrange your available filters. You can click the check sign on the right of each filter if you want it to be visible and uncheck the ones you prefer to hide.

The filters are what make the "wow factor" of INSTAGRAM because it enables you to manipulate the photo on the go.

## Lux

This is the sun-like symbol beside filters that allows you to balance the brightness and contrast of your photo.

## Tools

This is the tool sign after the LUX that offers more editing options such as ADJUST, BRIGHTNESS,

CONTRAST, WARMTH, SATURATION, COLOR, FADE, HIGHLIGHTS, SHADOWS, TILT SHIFT, and SHARPEN.

The options may overwhelmed you, but don't forget to make it balance and don't overdo it.

Don't forget to click the "check" sign at the right side above to apply your editing and click the "X" sign to undo. The "arrow" pointing to the right allow you to proceed and skip some options.

**Share A Photo**

You can share your INSTAGRAM post by clicking the OPTIONS at the right bottom of your post. This gives you the options to SHARE, EDIT, DELETE and COPY SHARE URL.

**Hashtag**

Hashtag is used to categorize or identify a post in a single topic.

Here are some popular hashtags that you can use.

**#TBT #ThrowbackThursday:** This can be your baby photo, your graduation photo or maybe your 8$^{th}$ birthday.

**#FlashbackFriday:** You can use this hashtag when you upload a photo of the late 90's, previous culture trends and 10 years ago photos of places.

### d. ACTIVITY

This shows the activities performed by the people you follow and by you.

### In The "Following" Section

It shows the photos liked by the people you follow and the new users that they started following. This makes easier for you to browse related niches.

### In The "You" Section

It shows your notifications such as the people who liked your photo, new users that started following you and special mentions from your followers. Remember that mentions are used to tag a specific person when you are conversing under a post. Don't forget to use mentions because they will not be notified.

When someone started following you the "PLUS USER" sign in the right side gives you the option to follow back the user.

### e. USER PROFILE

This is your personal profile where you can track how many posts have you've posted so far, how many followers and following you have.

On the right side above is the "OPTIONS" tab that allows you to perform other tasks to manage your account.

### 1. Follow People

This allows you to find, invite and connect friends from your other social networking sites.

### 2. Edit Your Account

This option allows you to manage your NAME, USERNAME, WEBSITE, BIO, EMAIL ADDRESS, PHONE NUMBER AND GENDER. You can change it from time to time; just make sure that you are using an active e-mail address and phone number so it will be easy for you to recover your password once you forgot it.

You can also, CHANGE YOUR PASSWORD, browse the POSTS YOU'VE LIKED and choose to make your account PRIVATE.

NOTE: Making your account private makes your posts only visible to your followers. Also, only people you approved will be able to follow you. However, this won't affect your existing followers.

## 3. Setting

You can optionally link your INSTAGRAM to your other social networking sites so that your posts will also visible to those linked accounts. It is like posting a photo or video in all your social networking sites by using only INSTAGRAM.

### Push Notifications

You can also manage the scope of your notifications by choosing among OFF, FROM PEOPLE I FOLLOW or FROM EVERYONE.

### Advanced Features

This allows you to USE INSTAGRAM'S ADVANCED CAMERA and USE HIGH-QUALITY IMAGE PROCESSING. However, it does not work on all devices.

### Cellular Data Use

This gives you the option to USE LESS DATE, however, this may affect your browsing and the quality of photos you upload.

### Auto-Save

By turning on the SAVE ORIGINAL PHOTOS and SAVE VIDEOS AFTER POSTING allows you to have a copy of your photos and videos on your phone.

NOTE: You can on and off this feature, just make sure that you have enough memory space to keep it.

### Support

This option directs you to HELP CENTER and allows you to REPORT A PROBLEM that you encountered.

### Blog

This displays handpicked INSTAGRAM ACCOUNTS that showcases different niches. You can also download INSTAGRAM BLOG to your IOS, ANDROID and WINDOWS devices. This is a great hub to enjoy and get inspired by photography and visual arts.

## f. INSTAGRAM DIRECT

This allows you to share a photo to selected followers only. You just have to click the "DIRECT" tab, click the "PLUS SIGN" button to add a photo and edit it as well, write a caption and then select the followers you wish to share the photo.

To continue or browse your "DIRECT", click on the tray icon on the right side top of the homepage.

NOTE: This picture will only be visible to the selected users and won't appear in the public newsfeed.

## g. INSTAGRAM VIDEO

To set the sound of your videos on and off, you can tap on the button on the bottom right. Then tap the options, it is the "3 vertical dots" at the right and choose between on and off.

If you are browsing other videos and you want to listen to its sound, just simply tap on the sound button located at the top right corner of the video.

There you go; you have successfully built your INSTAGRAM account. Perhaps, you are now thinking on how to make the most of it. You might also be thinking about how to gain more followers and gain more likes in your every post.

If that is what you are thinking, then you probably want to make an INSTAGRAM account that matters.

# Chapter 4. How To Build A Successful Instagram Account?

So you want to be a master of your niche and to have influence in INSTAGRAM? Then, keep in mind the following to become someone worth following for. Remember that an INSTAGRAM account that matters is not only base on how many followers you have, but having many followers can help you make an account that matters.

**TIPS TO GAIN MORE FOLLOWERS AND LIKES**

**a. PHOTO IS KING**

Before you chase hundreds of likes and thousands of followers, make sure that your account is something worth it. You have to focus on your content because your PHOTO and VIDEO will speak for you. Make sure to upload high quality and creative posts. Post photos that relate to you and something that will grab the attention and interest of your audience.

THINGS TO REMEMBER:

Knowledge won't hurt you so if you have time and really serious in making an INSTAGRAM account that matters, then read some photography books. You can also invest in good phones with a good camera or just simply master the light combination, rule of third and other basic photography principles.

Keep consistent with your posts, but you can upload something different from time to time as an icebreaker. Here are some suggestions to try.

1. A photo or video of what makes you inspired and happy lately.

2. A screenshot of your favorite or most active users. Use this 1 post to give thanks and appreciate your followers.

## b. KEEP YOUR CAPTION SIMPLE AND SHORT

Keep in mind that INSTAGRAM is a photo and video sharing application and not a book. It is all about the visuals, so you need to keep your caption simple and short but direct to the point. Let your photo or video to communicate your message.

You can make a story in INSTAGRAM, and you can use it by posting creative photos with compelling captions. Make your captions a minimum of 8 words and maximum of 15 words so that it won't be looking heavy in the eyes of your followers.

## c. USE PROPER HASHTAGS AND LOCATION

Use the proper hashtag so you will be easily indexed and searched by related niches. Try to look for the popular hashtag about your niche and tag your post there. Most users put the hashtag in the caption and it looks like a spam. The proper and most effective way to take advantage of the use of hashtags is to put it in the comment section.

Location or Geo mapping is also a good way to boost your visibility that is mostly used by food bloggers and travelers. You can use it by clicking the "add location" before publishing your post. You can also tag your photo to related people.

If you visited a restaurant, you can take a photo of the food or your family enjoying the meal and then tag the INSTAGRAM account of the restaurant. The restaurant may like it and can even give you a shoutout.

When posting a photo of your friends and cliques, don't forget to tag them. You can tag them by clicking "tag" before you upload your post.

NOTE: Too much can be annoying and that also applies to hashtags so use it properly.

**d. CREATE A PERSONALITY**

To create an amazing personality in INSTAGRAM that people will love to follow, you have to be unique and recognizable with your posts. To do this, you have to define your niche. It could be about coffee, stones, travel photography, architecture, books and anything you are passionate about. Just make sure that you can post regularly with your chosen topic.

Since, INSTAGRAM is all about visuals, make sure to use a single filter to all your post to keep it clean, united and pleasing to the human eye.

WHAT TO REMEMBER?

1. INVEST IN EMOTION:

Choose your account tone. Is it witty? Poetic? Funny? Dramatic? Candid? You have to decide. Remember that every day, there are millions of photos shared and to stand out, you must create a connection with your audience.

## 2. THERE ARE NO BOXES

In creating posts don't confine yourself with limitations and traditions. INSTAGRAM is being creative so you keep on experimenting and combining different appeals.

## e. LIKE OTHER PHOTOS AND COMMENT

No one loves a snob.

Like other posts and take advantage in the "explore button". See who follows other related niches and get to know other accounts. You don't need to compete with them, instead collaborate with them so you can learn new thing, tricks and tips.

By liking other photos, your account becomes more visible to other users, and may increase new profile traffic. Also, keep your posts engaging by conversing to your followers.

## f. FOLLOW YOUR FOLLOWERS

Aside from following related accounts, follow also your active and faithful followers. Keep them involve, and cooperate with them by exchanging ideas and opinions through likes and comments.

There are also popular tags such as #like4likes used that offer free likes and free followers which you can use. The only rule here is to support each other by exchanging likes, shoutouts and follows.

## g. BE ENGAGING

There are many ways to engage your followers and audience and here are some of them.

## 1. CALL TO ACTION

This is encouraging your audience to like and follow you in a creative way.

Examples:

Post a picture of your dream place. For example, a photo of street in Japan and then put a caption that encourages action such as:

"WOAH! I want to go the JAPAN. Like if you feel the same way."

Or post your photo of an event or concert you attended and put a caption saying,

"Best concert ever. Who else is in the event?"

## h. SYNC TO YOUR OTHER SOCIAL NETWORKING ACCOUNT

By linking your INSTAGRAM account in your other social networking sites, it will notify your more audience and future followers. This will also make it easier for them to find your account and follow you.

### i. POST STRATEGICALLY AND INTELIGENTLY.

To gain likes in your posts, you also need timing. Post your photo or video at the right time when most of your followers are online. Remember to study and understand the demographics of your users. For example, if your audience is mostly teenagers, posting around 6:30am on Saturday morning is lame. A more strategic move is to post around 12noon to afternoon where most teenagers are awake and online.

Also, take note to post regularly, but not too much. Instead of uploading 5 individual selfies, you can make a collage so you can put it in one post. To make a selfie collage, browse some photo editing applications in the app store.

SUGGESTIONS FOR BRANDS AND BUSINESSES:

If you are a business, you can download an application that analyzes the activity of your audience and the performance of your account.

## j. ASK FOR IT

You can ask for likes, follows and shoutouts without looking like a fame digger or a spam by asking it ethically. How? Start to list down related accounts, follow them, like and comment to their post.

EXAMPLE:

@1234567 Great gallery. I see that you are interested in surfing and I am also. Why don't we connect?

@abdefg What a cute cat you have. You might also be interested in cat fashion and pet grooming products. Check my account if you got time.

This is more appropriate and way more acceptable than commenting "Please Follow me". You can ask people to follow you by highlighting the reasons why they should. It can be because you have the same niche, you want to collaborate, you want to interview them for a blog post any many more.

## k. LAUNCH A CONTEST

Launching a contest can attract new followers and this is a good strategy to boost the online presence of your business. A contest doesn't need to be too complicated. Your goal here is to increase your visibility and to engage your target audience.

SAMPLE CONTEST you can use for your brand:

1. First 20,000 followers will receive 20% discount from selected items. Just like this photo, follow us, comment "I'M IN" below and tag 3 friends.

2. 10 lucky winners will win a trip to Hawaii. Just post a photo of you wearing your favorite hats from us. Don't forget to tag us and hashtag #HawaiianHatContestByNameOfBrandHere.

REMEMBER: Be sincere and honest. No one likes a liar so make sure that the contests that you launch are legit.

## l. EXPERIMENT

In a world where everyone is looking for fresh and new, your INSTAGRAM stardom can be achieve by starting a trend. Keep on experimenting in your photography, visual technics and captions. There is no single definite way to be popular in INSTAGRAM, so keep it real and let your personality stand out.

**m. HAVE FUN AND ENJOY**

INSTAGRAM is fun application that connects people through photographs in a creative way. Don't forget to have fun while you are building a strong INSTAGRAM account. It should be an extension of who are you as a person or the values of a brand and not just a business of collecting likes and followers.

## Final Words

To sum it all up, INSTAGRAM offers you an artistic way to capture moments of your daily lives. It is a powerful social networking site to let your ideas, thoughts, emotion and memories in a photo or video to go across the world. We know that pictures matters and it can communicate in its own. So whatever you post in your INSTAGRAM account, be responsible and entitled of it.

May you think before you click, may your post be more positive than negative and may it empower other people and not to humiliate them.

**Thank You Page**

I want to personally thank you for reading my book. I hope you found information in this book useful and I would be very grateful if you could leave your honest review about this book. I certainly want to thank you in advance for doing this.

If you have the time, you can check my other books too.

Lightning Source UK Ltd.
Milton Keynes UK
UKOW06f0036300716

279566UK00017B/473/P